Quick Callanetics

FOR YOUR HIPS AND BEHIND

T0315625

Quick Callanetics

For Your Hips and Behind

Callan Pinckney

First Published in 1992 by Vermilion, an imprint of Ebury Publishing
Ebury Publishing is a Random House Group Company
Random House
20 Vauxhall Bridge Road
London SW1V 2SA

Pinckney, Callan
    Quick callanetics - hips and behind: Firm up and
    fight the fat in only 20 minutes a day.
    I. Title
    613.7

    ISBN 9780091954833

Edited by Emma Callery
Designed by Clive Dorman
Typeset in Times New Roman by Clive Dorman

Printed and bound in Great Britain by Clays Ltd, St Ives plc

The Random House Group Limited supports The Forest Stewardship
Council® (FSC®), the leading international forest-certification organisation.
Our books carrying the FSC label are printed on FSC®-certified paper.
FSC is the only forest-certification scheme supported by the leading
environmental organisations, including Greenpeace. Our
paper procurement policy can be found at
www.randomhouse.co.uk/environment

CONTENTS

INTRODUCTION

Welcome to Quick Callanetics. Whether you regularly practise a Callanetics programme using a book, video, or an authorized class in one of our new studios, or you are experiencing Callanetics for the first time, this book will give you safe, fast and effective results if followed properly. By using the basic programme set out in the original book, millions of readers have already discovered that Callanetics is a safe and quick way to change bodyshape to give the firm, attractive body we all dream about. Those mastering that programme have graduated to *Super Callanetics*. *Callanetics Countdown* presents a shorter programme for those with more demanding time schedules and if you are seeking a more gradual introduction to the basic Callanetics one-hour programme. *Callanetics for Your Back* is for those people with backaches or back problems. The book is designed to correct the problem or to make the back more flexible and to release pain. The exercises are also preventative for those who don't have back problems and never want to have them as the stretches and contractions actually strengthen the back. The appeal has proven to be international, with books now published in many countries around the world.

The huge success of the first Callanetics book brought a demand for videos; which include the original *Callanetics: Ten Years Younger in Ten Hours*, followed by *Beginning Callanetics* and *Super Callanetics*. Now we have the new *Quick Callanetics* series with three 20-minute workout tapes for the legs, stomach, and hips and behind. This book contains all the exercises, and more, as featured in *Quick Callanetics: Hips and Behind*.

We all share common problems and have as our goal a strong, firm and shapely body, but our bodies also differ in various ways. A person may have a special problem in one area and much less of a problem elsewhere. This book is written in response to those of you who may require extra attention to the hips and buttocks, or, as Americans prefer to call it, the behind. Here is a programme designed purely to counteract the effect of gravity tugging at our behind, causing it to droop, sag and spread. By using this book to concentrate on your hips and behind, you will soon firm up the muscles, making those saddlebags disappear and change a gooshy pear-shape to the perfect peach we all long to have.

Note that when the bottom starts to pull in and up, you will experience a lump on both sides of the bottom just below the waist. Don't let this frighten you as it did me at first. Remember it has taken years for this drooping spread to occur. In no time at all this area will smooth out to shape your bottom like a child's. For some people, when doing the bottom exercises for the first few times you may feel a sensation in the hip. This should disappear as the muscles become stronger.

THE ORIGINS OF CALLANETICS

I grew up in the deep South of the United Sates, Georgia to be exact, born of a long line of Pinckneys whose ancestors include the first Viscount of Surrey. They fought with William the Conqueror in the Norman Invasion in 1066. I found a life of well-bred tradition restricting, but not so the Pinckney fighting spirit. And I had to fight from the beginning for I was born with curvature of the spine caused by scoliosis and I had to wear steel leg braces for seven years to correct my club feet. It was only twelve years of ballet classes which helped to turn my feet outward.

After two years of college I decided to explore the world, going first to Europe and then setting off to explore Africa, Asia and finally the Far East. I worked hard doing manual labour to make ends meet, and I further damaged my already abused body by carrying a backpack that almost equalled my weight, doing much of my travelling by foot. At 5' 1", I had always been petite. The starchy foods, such as digestive biscuits, and 40 cups of heavily sugared tea a day in England pushed my weight up to 129lb (9st 3lb). I developed a middle-age spread. Later my weight dropped to 78lb (5st 8lb) as a result of amoebic dysentery contracted during my travels. I lost muscle tone. I strained my back and knees, and my behind sagged and spread, making my outer thighs look like saddlebags.

Returning to the United States after eleven years, my physical condition was desperate. I had been told earlier by doctors that if I didn't have immediate surgery on my back and knees I could spend the rest of my life in a wheelchair. I could not allow this to happen, but I was unwilling to face the possibility of scarring from surgery. Within a year I could barely get out of bed.

DEVELOPING CALLANETICS

In the exercise classes I started attending on my return to the States I was shocked that most of them put a strain on the back. The movements were impossible for me, so I began to develop exercises to accommodate my physical condition. During my travels I had experienced a great number of exercise techniques, including belly dancing in the Middle East, and I remembered my earlier ballet training. Gradually I evolved a slow, gentle way to position my body into movements which protected the back. Instead of applying pressure to the lower back, I developed exercises which stretched the spine. At the same time, they penetrated deep into the body to reach muscles and shape and tone them with amazing speed. I learnt that the circular motions used in belly dancing loosened the pelvic area, gradually allowing movements in the sacrum area (lower back) where I had no flexibility left.

Each motion was delicate and precise, involving ¼ to ½ inch – tiny movements were all my body was capable of doing at the time. But these tiny motions focused the muscles in a remarkable way. In addition to correcting my physical problems, I noticed my behind pulling up and in, my stomach flattening, my posture improving dramatically day by day, my thighs becoming firm and youthful along with my inner thighs and underarms. I no longer wobbled when I walked and my arms did not jiggle when I waved. I felt totally comfortable in shorts or a sleeveless dress. My body was becoming incredibly strong and felt years younger. Friends noticed the change in my body. They wanted to know my secret. I showed them my exercises, and they also got the same, safe, quick results.

THE FIRST CALLANETICS BOOK

For the next eleven years I taught small classes of students who had heard about my exercises from their friends. My students had noticed remarkable changes in their bodies. For lack of a name for my exercises, my students named them 'Callanetics', and they also said it made their bodies feel 'ten years younger in ten hours'. They encouraged me to write a book. Finally, I called an agent. The book was a hard one to sell, I was told. I was not a celebrity, model or movie star. And it seemed that at the time every celebrity, model and movie star in the world had an exercise book on the market. Furthermore, I was not aerobic and aerobics were in vogue. But the agent was convinced by my exercises, just as my students had been, and the book was eventually sold to a publisher for a very modest advance.

Then came the crushing news. Of the few thousand books printed and distributed, over half had been returned unsold. I was too unknown. The publisher was to abandon the book and sell the remaining copies at cost. However, I knew that if I could only reach the public, they would recognize the value of my programme and reap the benefits of Callanetics just as my students had done. I did everything I could think of to bring the book to the attention of the public. When I went to Chicago for a final television appearance, magic happened and 14 months of hard work promoting the book paid off. As a result of that single television appearance, enough copies were sold in a week to place the book on *The New York Times* bestseller list in the number two position. It remained on the list for almost a year. That success has now been repeated in many other countries including Britain. I will be forever grateful to all those people who brought Callanetics to the attention of the public. And I am grateful to all of you who told your friends of the great results achieved through Callanetics.

CALLANETICS TODAY

Today, those of you who practise Callanetics are legion with more continuously joining the ranks. As this is being written, the word 'Callanetics' is entering the language through the *Collins English Dictionary* which defines Callanetics as 'a system of exercise involving repetition of small muscular movements and contractions, designed to improve muscle tone.' And what brought all this about? The answer is simple: RESULTS. The programme works for anyone of any age giving the fastest results in the shortest time with no injuries.

When I launched the original Callanetics programme, I introduced myself as a teacher. At the time the video was released I was 47 years old. Well, time marches on and I am now 52, and I am still a teacher. Now I teach Master Teachers who teach others. Callanetics has grown enormously from the days when I taught small, private classes in my small studio on New York's mid-East Side.

In November 1990, another major chapter in the story of Callanetics started with the opening of the Callanetics Franchise Corporation with headquarters in Denver, Colorado. Since the introduction of the books and videos, I was deluged with requests for classes and qualified Callanetics teachers. It became obvious that a programme for training and certifying instructors to teach Callanetics was needed. This was especially so in light of reports that classes were being offered by unauthorized persons with no assurance that the exercises were being taught safely or effectively. Now, however, you can receive qualified instruction throughout the United States and several other countries including Great Britain, Belgium, Mexico and Australia, with teachers who have been properly trained and are certified. You will find further information on how to find classes or how to open your own studio at the beginning of this book. I urge you to seek instruction only from those studios who document their certification and are listed by the Callanetics Franchise Corporation.

ADVERSE REACTIONS

I am very annoyed when Callanetics is attacked by those who have not tried the programme and cannot speak first hand of its safety and benefits. The same is true of other so-called exercise experts who feel it necessary to protect their interests by being critical of Callanetics.

Rather than pointing out what other programmes can't and don't do and the injury they can cause, I have always maintained the positive value that my programmes can give. I have always said, 'My only competition is plastic surgery', and that is still true.

Using Quick Callanetics

You may use this book in several ways. It is small and compact and can travel with you from home to work, on business trips or vacations, or wherever you choose to give yourself a quick reminder of the steps of the programme. If you are taking Callanetics classes in an authorized studio, you can use this book as a brush up source between classes. If you use an audio or video tape, this book will freeze the motion with a written explanation of how the movements work and will help you fix the precision of the position.

The book is divided into easy-to-follow sections. First there is the Quick Callanetics programme, exactly following the routine on the video. This is followed by some Advanced Exercises for those of you who may wish to push themselves a little further. Should you find the Quick Callanetics programme too difficult at first, the Build Your Strength section will soon enable you to work through the exercises with ease. Please note that some of the photographs in this book show you the ultimate goal of Callanetics. Do not worry if you can't do the same immediately—always work at your own pace.

Triple slow motion

The movements in Callanetics are tiny, delicate, gentle, and precise. They are done very slowly, as I have always said 'in triple slow motion'. Think of Callanetics as meditation in motion. In this way you reach deep, deep into the body to work the large muscles, as though working through them layer by layer. Never jerk and never bounce. Know how tiny ¼ to ½ of an inch is. Measure it! The movement is a pulse. If the directions call for 25 repetitions, think of it as 25 pulses. Do that amount of movement slowly and gently. Only when you are aware of the smallness and the gentleness of the movements, are you ready to do Callanetics correctly. You will then find your muscles will perform at the level they are best able to. Don't be upset if you have to take frequent breaks or if you can only do a few repetitions at first. You will be surprised at how much stronger you will become in very little time.

No forcing

Because it is so important, let me emphasise that you must not force. If you are stretching, your muscles will only stretch at their capacity and you should not force them beyond that level. While you are contracting, or strengthening, the muscles, you should not be able to do more repetitions than the muscles will allow at that particular time. This prevents you from forcing the muscles beyond their limitations. Forcing the muscles can result in exhaustion or injury.

Do not – I repeat – do not be distressed or disappointed if you can only do two or three repetitions at the beginning, this is a natural process. With each session you will become stronger, and you will be able to do more. The most important goal is to learn to protect and respect your back to prevent back pain and to relieve back problems.

Curling up the pelvis

If there is one motion that is the key to Callanetics, it is curling up the pelvis, the link between the upper and lower body. Tighten your buttocks, and in triple slow motion try to move, or 'curl up', the pelvic area, as if you were trying to bring your pubic bone to your naval. Imagine there is a length of string attached to the bottom of your leotard. Gently pull straight up on the string and your pelvis will curl up. This movement stretches your spine, and strengthens your abdominal, inner- and front-thigh, and buttock muscles, as well as your calves and feet, if you are standing. Gaining freedom in the pelvic area is very important because it affects posture, balance, and alignment of the body. It also loosens the hip joints and allows for more fluid movements. The more the pelvis is curled up, the deeper the buttock muscles contract and the faster the results.

Breathing

Always try to breathe naturally - and remember to breathe! Many people actually forget to breathe when exercising.

Counting

Several of the exercises include instructions to 'hold for a count of ...' You should count 'one thousand and one, one thousand and two,' etc. If you count aloud, the added plus is that you will be sure to breathe!

Think relaxation

Don't tense the body. Let the gentleness control the motion. By not forcing you will gain the full benefits of an exercise without exhausting the muscles or yourself. In the behind exercises you will find me telling you to relax the legs and the feet. Exert the minimum amount of effort for maximum results. This is not to say you will not feel the exercises. You will feel them working deep in specific areas, without straining other parts of the body, particularly the back.

Commitment

Think, 'This is my time – a time I give to myself.' Think beautiful, soft thoughts; allow yourself to visualize and fantasize. You have done more than enough for everyone else. Now it is your turn. You will eventually attach the same importance to yourself as you do to the other aspects of your life. Because it is fast and effective, Callanetics will fit into any schedule and can be done anywhere as it does not require special equipment. Just 20 minutes a day will produce results you will be extremely proud of. The other books in the series deal with the legs and the stomach.

This programme is designed just for you. So let's get started. You'll be surprised how quickly you will see results and be capable of doing the required repetitions with ease. And remember, *gentleness* is the key word.

QUICK CALLANETICS

THE FOLLOWING EXERCISES:
• RESCULPT THE BEHIND •
• ROUND AND LIFT THE BUTTOCKS
TO LOOK LIKE A PERFECT PEACH SHAPE •
• RESTORE FIRMNESS •
• ELIMINATE SADDLEBAGS •

PLEASE NOTE: This series of exercises may appear complicated at first. Please be sure to read through the text to get an understanding of what you must do before attempting them. The benefits will be well worth it. Don't worry about doing these exercises at exactly the level shown in the photographs. Do them at your own level, which is perfect for you. If you can only do five pulses at first, that is your level. As your muscles strengthen, your form will improve. Don't be discouraged, you will be able to do more repetitions each time you do the exercises. You'll be working the muscles deeper and deeper, and in no time at all each exercise will be a breeze. It is advisable not to wear shoes for any of these exercises; the weight of them is simply too heavy.

REMEMBER:
• NO BOUNCING •
• NO JERKING •
• NO FORCING •
• WORK AT YOUR OWN PACE •
• ALWAYS TAKE BREATHERS IF NECESSARY •
• GENTLENESS IS THE KEY TO THESE EXERCISES •

Up and Down

THIS EXERCISE:
- STRETCHES THE SPINE •
- LOOSENS THE KNEES •

TECHNIQUE

❏ Stand with your feet a hip-width apart. Stretch both your arms up to the ceiling as high as you can. Tighten your buttocks, and curl your pelvis up (see page 14). Now stretch even more. Relax your knees—don't lock them—and keep your feet flat on the floor.

❏ In one smooth motion, gently bend your knees as much as you can, and lower your upper body towards the floor, with your arms reaching forward. Imagine you are trying to grasp an object on the floor in front of you. Your torso is stretching out and away.

❏ Gently swing your arms back, raising them as high as you can behind your body. Your knees will straighten slightly and your buttocks will raise with the motion of your arms going to the back and then up.

NOTE: When you have swung your arms back, as above, this will be one of the few instances where your pelvis will not be curled up.

❏ Just as you are about to reverse the motion to go back up to your starting position, tighten your buttocks and curl your pelvis up even more than you think you can. Keep it curled up until you return, arms once again stretching up towards the ceiling. If you have a swayback, tip your pelvis up as much as you can.

Repetitions
WORK UP TO 5

DON'TS

❏ Do not arch your back while stretching your arms up to the ceiling.

❏ Do not tense your knees or feet.

❏ Do not tense your shoulders or neck.

The Neck Relaxer

THIS EXERCISE:
- LOOSENS THE NECK AND SHOULDERS •
- STRETCHES THE SPINE •
- INCREASES JOINT FLEXIBILITY •
- RELEASES TENSION IN THE NECK AND BETWEEN THE SHOULDER BLADES •

❑ Stand erect, feet a hip-width apart. Relax your shoulders and bend your knees. Tighten your buttocks, and curl your pelvis up more than you think you can.

❑ In triple slow motion, roll your head down, resting your chin on your chest.

❑ Still slowly, move your chin over to your right shoulder as far as you can.

❑ Then aim your chin up towards the ceiling as high as you can, at the same time stretching the back of your neck up.

❑ Delicately bring your chin back down to your chest.

❑ Gently move your chin over your left shoulder, and then stretch it up as high as it will go.

❑ Bring it back down to where your chin touches your chest again. This is one repetition.

Repetitions
TO EACH SIDE

3

TECHNIQUE

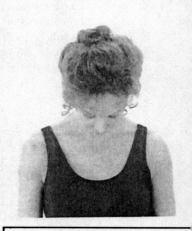

DON'TS

❑ **Do not make any harsh or sudden movements.**

❑ **Do not hunch or tense your shoulders.**

❑ **Do not tense your jaw.**

❑ **Do not lock your knees.**

❑ **Do not stick out your stomach or arch your lower back.**

Bringing Up the Rear (Sitting)

THE NEXT TWO EXERCISES:

- SCULPT THE BUTTOCKS, GIVING THEM
A 'PRECIOUS PEACH' (INSTEAD
OF A 'SAGGING PEAR') SHAPE •
- • GET RID OF THE 'JIGGLE' •
- • REDUCE SADDLEBAGS, AND EVENTUALLY MAKE
THEM DISAPPEAR •
- • STRENGTHEN THE ARM MUSCLES •

NOTE: The barre used in the following exercises could be made from almost any piece of sturdy furniture such as a sofa or chair. Choose a height that is comfortable for you.

TECHNIQUE

❏ Sitting on the floor or on a mat to cushion yourself if necessary, place your left knee bent in front of you with your left foot 8-10 inches away from your body. Your right knee is bent and even with your right hip. Your right foot rests on the floor behind you.

❏ Put your left hand on the barre. Making sure that your right hip remains facing the barre, use your right hand to roll your right hip forward as far as you can. As the hip is rolled forward, the torso automatically turns to the left. Your foot should come off the floor. If it doesn't, you can assist with your hand. Put your right hand back on the barre.

21

❑ Lift your right knee off the floor no more than 3 inches. Keep your right hip rolled forward and your torso straight and relaxed. Put your right hand on the barre.

❑ Pulse your knee in triple slow motion back and forth, $\frac{1}{4}$ to $\frac{1}{2}$ inch.

❑ Try to relax your entire body, even though at first you will be holding on to the barre for dear life. Repeat this exercise on the opposite side.

❑ At first, you might have to lean over to the opposite side of the leg you are working in order to be able to lift your knee off the floor. Or you can rest your hand on the floor to support your torso. Eventually you will be able to sit perfectly erect without support.

Repetitions
TO EACH SIDE
WORK UP TO 100

NOTE: The more your hip is rolled forward for these first two sitting exercises (and the Out to the Side [Kneeling] exercise), the more you will be working your buttocks muscles. If you have a swayback, always round your upper back as much as you can, or, if you feel it's necessary to protect your back, you can also let your torso lean over to the opposite side of the leg being used. This will stretch the spine even more and take the pressure off your lower back.

REMEMBER:
Gentleness is the key word. Relax into the floor and take a breather whenever you feel in need of one. Work at your own pace.

IF YOU WANT MORE OF A WORKOUT FOR YOUR BUTTOCKS:
Lower your foot a little bit, and aim your kneecap towards the ceiling, but do not let your hip rotate to the back. For even more of a workout in this same position, you can also lift your knee and foot a wee bit more.

WHEN THIS EXERCISE BECOMES TOO EASY:
Be sure to sit more erect. You can also raise your barre, or place your hands higher up on your piece of furniture. The higher the barre, the more intense this exercise becomes.

IF YOU FEEL IT'S TOO MUCH, AND YOUR BODY IS BEGINNING TO TENSE UP:
Take a breather, then roll back into position. You can also switch sides, but be sure to do a proper count for both sides before continuing this section.

NOTE: At first it will seem impossible for most people to lift the knee off the floor, much less pulse the leg ¼ to ½ inch. When your muscles become extremely strong, you'll be able to roll your hip forward even more, causing your knee to be so low that it will almost seem to be brushing the floor. You will soon not need to use your hand to roll your hip forward.

23

DON'TS

❏ Do not arch your lower back.

❏ Do not push your stomach forward or out. This will arch your back.

❏ Do not tense your legs.

❏ Do not tense your neck.

❏ Do not allow the movements back and forth to become more than barely perceptible.

❏ Do not allow the foot of your working leg to rest on the floor. If it starts to feel heavy, take a breather.

❏ Do not hunch your shoulders.

❏ Do not allow your torso to push forward when you are rolling your hip forward. This will put pressure on your lower back. Keep your torso erect but relaxed.

❏ Do not take the knee of your working leg past your hip when you are returning forward during the little motions.

❏ Do not let your hips become uneven.

❏ Do not forget to relax even more!

NOTE: If you feel pressure on your lower back, you have four choices:
  Round your upper back;
  Lean over to the opposite side of your working leg just as much as you have to, keeping your back straight;
  Place your hand on the floor to support your torso; or
  When nothing else works, tighten your buttocks and curl your pelvis up.

Out to the Side (Sitting)

TECHNIQUE

❏ Still seated, place your left hand on the barre and bend your left leg out on the floor in front of you. Relax your shoulders.

❏ Fully extend your right leg out, straight, directly to the side, even with your hip. Place your right hand on your right hip and then slowly roll your right hip and leg over so that the tops of your toes are aiming into the floor (if possible). Put your right hand on the barre.

❏ Bring your right leg in towards your body. Because your right leg can move in 3 to 4 inches, this will automatically take your hips to the left, causing you to lean slightly to the left.

❏ Lift your foot no more than 3 inches.

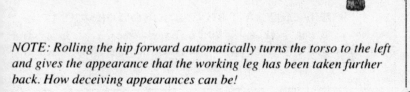

NOTE: Rolling the hip forward automatically turns the torso to the left and gives the appearance that the working leg has been taken further back. How deceiving appearances can be!

❑ Gently pulse your right foot up and down, ¼ to ½ inch. The movement can remain so small because the hip has been rolled over so much.

❑ Repeat this exercise on the opposite side.

Repetitions
TO EACH SIDE
WORK UP TO **100**

WHEN THIS EXERCISE BECOMES TOO EASY:
Take your working leg to the back without rotating your hip back. You can also sit more erect, and roll your hip further forward.

IF THIS EXERCISE IS BECOMING TOO DIFFICULT:
Slowly ease your working leg forward a few inches. You can also lean directly over to the opposite side or bend your knee. Take breathers whenever you have to.

DON'TS

❑ **Do not lock your knee, but keep your extended leg very straight.**

❑ **Do not allow your torso to push forward. This will put pressure on your lower back.**

❑ **Do not allow your working hip to roll back, keep it forward as much as you can.**

❑ **Do not arch your back.**

❑ **Do not continue if you feel pressure on your lower back. Instead you have four choices:**

Round your upper back;

Lean over to the opposite side of your working leg as much as you need to;

Place your hand on the floor to support your torso; or

Tighten your buttocks and curl your pelvis up more than you think you can.

NOTE: If you are in the most advanced position for this exercise, you will only be able to lift your foot no more than 1 inch. If you are not yet strong enough for this, you may lean your torso as much as you need to to the left and lift your leg higher—but make sure it is no higher than 3 inches off the floor. Otherwise, because you may be tired, you might turn your leg towards the ceiling, and begin working the front thigh muscles instead of the buttocks.

Bringing Up the Rear (Kneeling)

Even though I know I keep saying 'Round your upper back', when your muscles become strong enough and you can do the famous pelvic curl-up as second nature, many of you will have noticed that you no longer have to round your upper back during these kneeling exercises.

THE NEXT TWO EXERCISES:

- STRENGTHEN THE SAME AREAS AS THE FIRST TWO, PLUS •
- STRENGTHEN THE KNEELING (NON-WORKING) THIGH •
- STRENGTHEN THE HAMSTRING AND CALF OF BOTH LEGS •

NOTE: People who have swaybacks must learn to curl the pelvis up even more to stop their lower back from arching. This prevents irritation. Don't forget to protect your knees with a towel or mat.

TECHNIQUE

❏ Kneel, with knees together and both hands resting loosely on your barre or piece of furniture, elbows slightly bent. Stretch your torso up and then lean back until your arms are straight. Round your upper back to stretch your spine and relax your shoulders. Tighten your buttocks, and curl your pelvis up.

❏ In triple slow motion, without lifting your hip, take your right knee out to the side and up towards the ceiling as high as it can go without lifting your right foot, letting it slide across the floor.

❏ When your knee will not go up any further, take your foot up off the floor no more than 2 inches. Curl your pelvis up still more and relax your shoulders.

❏ Take your left hip towards the left very slightly to distribute your weight off your kneecap.

❏ Keep your buttocks directly over, or above, your knees.

❏ The more the pelvis is curled up, the deeper the buttock muscles contract producing faster results.

NOTE: Whenever you tighten your buttocks and curl your pelvis up, your working leg will automatically come forward. Be sure to take your working knee back, allowing it to be even with your kneeling knee, to get the full benefit of this exercise. The fact that you're taking your knee back does not mean that the hip of that same leg has to move! Be sure, however, that your pelvis stays curled up.

H I P S & B E H I N D

❏ Gently move your right knee back and forth, no more than ¼ to ½ inch.

❏ Repeat this exercise on the opposite side. Take breathers whenever you need to.

Repetitions
TO EACH SIDE
WORK UP TO 100

NOTE: Looking closely at the angle of the left foot, you can tell how much my foot has been rotated to the right. To start with, keep the kneeling leg directly behind you. When you become strong, you will be able to take your foot of the kneeling leg to the right.

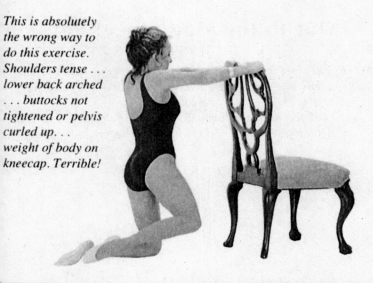

This is absolutely the wrong way to do this exercise. Shoulders tense . . . lower back arched . . . buttocks not tightened or pelvis curled up. . . weight of body on kneecap. Terrible!

DON'TS

❏ Do not be lazy with your pelvis, really curl it up more than you think you can.

❏ Do not bend your arms.

❏ Do not tense your back and buttocks. Always make sure that your lower back is straight and relaxed, and that your buttocks are not sticking out.

❏ Do not slump or aim your buttocks towards the floor.

❏ Do not continue if you feel pressure on your lower back. Instead, round your upper back even more.

❏ Do not move your hip when taking your working leg back and forth. Aim with your knee, going back and forth in tiny little movements. Try to keep your knee aimed up towards the ceiling, and don't let it go in front of the line of your left knee.

❏ Do not hunch your shoulders. Relax by keeping them rounded.

❏ Do not put your weight on your kneecap. Shift your weight to ensure it is off this sensitive part of your body.

Out to the Side (Kneeling)

NOTE: The more the pelvis is curled up, the less the foot will come off the floor and the more the buttocks muscles will be working for faster results.
At first it will feel as if your foot will never lift off the floor. Just keep trying and all of a sudden it will happen.

TECHNIQUE

❏ Kneeling, with both hands on your barre or piece of furniture, lean your torso back until your arms are straight and relaxed. Stretch your right leg straight out to the side, even with your hip.

❏ Rotate your right leg forward, until the top of your toes rest on the floor, if possible.

❏ Tighten your buttocks, and curl your pelvis up more than you ever thought you could. Round your upper back. Make sure your lower back is straight, not arched, and relaxed.

❏ Allowing your hips to move to the left, bring your right leg in towards your body so that you won't be putting pressure on your kneecap.

NOTE: Because of the angle of the chair in this photograph, it appears that I have taken the right leg back. The leg here is actually even with the hip.

❑ Curl your pelvis up again and then gently lift your right foot, up and down, in a smooth and tiny motion, no more than 3 inches off the floor.

❑ Repeat this exercise on the opposite side. Remember to take a breather whenever necessary.

Repetitions
TO EACH SIDE
WORK UP TO 100

IF THIS EXERCISE IS BECOMING TOO DIFFICULT:

Take a breather. If your working leg is starting to feel too heavy, take it a wee bit forward. You can also lean your torso over, with your spine straight, to the side opposite your working leg. Remember to breathe naturally. If you do take a breather, be sure to get into the original starting position before continuing the exercise.

DON'TS

❏ Do not arch your lower back; keep it perfectly straight. Keep the top of your back rounded, as if you were a cat.

❏ Do not be lazy with your pelvis, keep it curled up more than you think you can, and keep your hips even.

❏ Do not tense your body: try to relax as much as you can, from head to toe, especially your shoulders and neck.

❏ Do not lock your knee but keep your working leg straight, relaxing your knee.

❏ Do not slump or aim your buttocks towards the floor.

❏ Do not ever place your full weight directly on your kneecap. Place a towel or exercise mat under your knee, if you like.

❏ Do not let your buttocks go behind your kneeling leg.

❏ Do not stick out your buttocks.

The Spine Stretch

Take advantage of this spine stretch as much as you can.

THIS EXERCISE:

• STRETCHES THE ENTIRE BACK, SPINE, BETWEEN THE SHOULDER BLADES, PECTORALS, BUTTOCKS, HIPS, AND OUTER THIGHS •

TECHNIQUE

❏ Lie on the floor, feet a hip-width apart, knees aiming towards the sky.

❏ Bending from the elbows, place your forearms at a right angle to the side of your head, resting them lightly with your palms facing upwards. Your wrists might not touch the floor, but your elbows should always remain on the floor.

❏ In triple slow motion, lift your right knee, bent, up to your chest. Let your left leg gently ease down until it rests on the floor.

Repetitions
TO EACH SIDE
WORK UP TO 50

FOR MORE OF A STRETCH:
Gently move your right knee up to your left elbow.

FOR EVEN MORE OF A STRETCH:
Ease your straight leg to the back of you, as shown in the photo above.

❏ Keeping both elbows on the floor, take your bent right knee over to your left side, away from your body as much as you can. Slowly move your knee and leg up and down ¼ to ½ inch.

❏ Gravity will bring your foot and knee nearer to the ground and eventually your foot and then your knee will be resting on the floor.

❏ To come out of this stretch and to go over to the other side, in triple slow motion, keeping your right knee bent, bring it back to your chest and then place your right foot on the floor, with your knee bent.

❏ Bend your left knee to your chest, and then slide your right foot down to the floor. This is all done in one smooth, continuous motion.

❏ Repeat this stretch on the opposite side.

❏ To come out of this stretch, in triple slow motion, keeping your left knee bent, bring it back to your chest, and then place your left foot on the floor. Bend your right knee, and place that foot flat on the floor. Then ease yourself up to a standing position by rolling over on to your side and easing yourself up gently using your arms.

DON'TS

❏ Do not force your bent leg down to the floor.

❏ Do not lift your shoulders or elbows off the floor.

❏ Do not tense your body, especially your neck.

❏ Do not force anything. Remember, gravity is doing the work, not you!

Coming Up off the Floor

One of the worst things you can do for your back is to jerk yourself up off the floor and just get up. It is very simple to learn how to get up gracefully, in a fluid, easy motion.

❏ Lying on the floor, with your knees bent and relaxed, gently roll your torso and your bent knees over to the right.

❏ Now place your hands on the floor over to your right side, and, in triple slow motion, ease yourself up gently to a sitting position.

❑ Then, using the strength of your arms, bring yourself up to a kneeling position. In triple slow motion, take your left leg up, bent, to where your left foot is resting on the floor. Do not lock your elbows.

❑ Bring your right leg up. Tighten your behind and curl your pelvis up. Then gently, straightening up one vertebra at a time, return to a standing position.

ADVANCED EXERCISES

Once you have mastered the Quick Callanetics programme you may find you have time to add a few more exercises to your daily 20-minute workout.

There are plenty of exercises in this section from which you can pick and choose. Bringing Up the Rear (Standing) and Out to the Side (Standing) work your hips, outer thighs (saddlebags) and buttock muscles even more. The Pelvic Rotation, Scoop and Figure of 8 also work the buttocks and leg muscles while at the same time allowing you to further increase your ability to curl your pelvis up even more. The Front-Thigh Stretch will stretch your front-thigh muscles to prevent them from bulking, giving them a long, lean look. These exercises are a fine addition to the Quick Callanetics programme, giving you more strength when working on the exercises aimed at assisting the hips and behind.

The Build Your Strength programme beginning on page 54 shows how to slowly increase your strength to work up to these exercises if you should find them too difficult at first.

REMEMBER:

If at any time you should find these exercises too difficult, stop for a breather. Always work at your own pace.

Bringing Up the Rear (Standing)

This exercise was drawn from a position in classical ballet called an attitude.

THE NEXT TWO EXERCISES:

- SCULPT THE BUTTOCKS, GIVING THEM
A 'PRECIOUS PEACH' SHAPE •
- GET RID OF 'JIGGLE' •
- REDUCE SADDLEBAGS, AND EVENTUALLY MAKE
THEM DISAPPEAR •
- STRENGTHEN THE ENTIRE STANDING LEG •
- STRENGTHEN THE HAMSTRING AND CALF OF
BOTH LEGS •
- STRETCH THE SPINE •

TECHNIQUE

❑ Stand at your barre or sturdy piece of furniture, your hands resting lightly on it for balance, elbows bent. Your feet are together.

❑ In triple slow motion, lift your right foot off the floor bending the knee, keeping it even with the opposite leg. Take it up and out to the side as high as you can without moving your right hip up or forward. Keep your right knee even with your left knee by not allowing the right knee to go forward or behind the left knee.

❑ Point your foot to the rear, and keep it relaxed. It should always be lower than your knees.

❑ Bend your left knee slightly, the one you're standing on. Tighten your buttocks, and curl your pelvis up. Round your upper back. Your knee may go forward, so carefully take it back, even with the opposite knee—but don't move your hip.

IF THIS EXERCISE IS TOO DIFFICULT:
Bring the working knee slightly forward.

❏ Bend sideways at the waist and aim your right shoulder towards the floor. Relax your shoulders and neck.

❏ Keeping your pelvis curled up as much as you can, rotate your knee up towards the ceiling, again without moving your hip. Then gently move your knee back and forth ¼ to ½ inch.

❏ Repeat this exercise on the opposite side.

DON'TS

❏ Do not arch your back at all. Make sure your lower back is stretched.

❏ Do not allow your hips to become uneven. Keep them parallel to the barre.

❏ Do not tense your shoulders or your neck.

❏ Do not lock your knees.

❏ Do not straighten the leg you're standing on, it should always be slightly bent.

NOTE: Keep the upper back rounded and to the side, and the arms relaxed. The left leg should be bent and relaxed as well. Always curl up the pelvis as much as you can.

REMEMBER:

The hip does not move when the knee is pulsing ¼ to ½ inch.

Repetitions
TO EACH SIDE

WORK UP TO 100

Out to the Side (Standing)

This exercise was also drawn from a position in classical
ballet called an arabesque.

TECHNIQUE

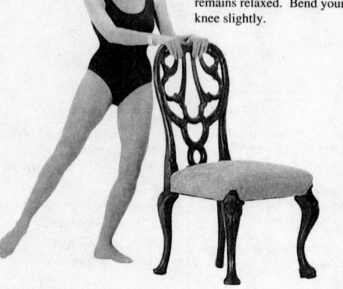

❏ Stand at your barre or piece of
furniture, your hands resting lightly
on it for balance, elbows bent.
Your feet are together.

❏ Take your right leg directly out
to the side, even with your hip,
pointing your toes like a ballet
dancer's but keeping them relaxed.
The toes should be aiming forward.
Your leg is straight, but your leg
remains relaxed. Bend your left
knee slightly.

*NOTE: This is one exercise I definitely take advantage of while standing
having a conversation with someone. When you become stronger, you
will not have to hold on to anything! The movement is so ridiculously
tiny that no one ever knows I'm even doing it. At that level, you should
keep your torso straight and relaxed.*

❏ Allowing your hips to move to the left, bring your right leg in towards your body. It can usually come in about 4 to 6 inches.

❏ Tighten your buttocks and curl your pelvis up.

❏ Bend at the waist and aim your right shoulder towards the floor. Relax your neck and shoulders.

❏ Tighten your buttocks and curl your pelvis up even more than you think you can.

❏ Gently start moving your foot up and down, ¼ to ½ inch.

❏ Repeat this exercise on the opposite side.

IF THIS EXERCISE IS TOO DIFFICULT AT FIRST:

Bend the working leg slightly, or take the working leg forward a bit. You can do both if necessary.

Repetitions
TO EACH SIDE

WORK UP TO 100

DON'TS

❏ Do not tense your shoulders; they should be doing absolutely nothing.

❏ Do not move your hips and keep them even.

❏ Do not arch your back.

❏ Do not let your pelvis go, always keep it curled up more than you think you can.

❏ Do not lose your position. If you feel that this is happening or that your arms are taking over, take a breather. Or take the working leg forward a wee bit.

❏ Do not lock your knees, but keep your working leg straight.

The Pelvic Rotation

NOTE: If you have knee problems, you can do the Pelvic Rotations in a standing position with your knees bent You will not see results as quickly, but as you already know , your health and safety are far more important! In the next two exercises most people with knee problems have experienced wonderful results.

THIS EXERCISE:

- STRENGTHENS THE BUTTOCKS, THIGHS, INNER THIGHS, LOWER BACK, STOMACH, AND PELVIC MUSCLES •
- STRETCHES THE ARMS AND SPINE •
- LOOSENS THE PELVIC AREA •

TECHNIQUE

❏ On a mat, sit comfortably on your heels. Your knees are together and your legs relaxed.

❏ Stretch your arms up over your head and clasp your hands together. Keep your torso erect, and feel the stretch in your back.

❏ Lift your torso 3 inches up off your heels. If you find resting in this position difficult, lift your torso further up until you are comfortable.

❏ If you feel pressure on your calves, lean your torso forward a little bit.

❑ Take your right hip over to the right side side as far as you can. Roll your pelvis forward, to the front, at the same time curling it up and aiming it in to your navel. Move your left hip over to the left side as far as you can. Then move your buttocks to the back, completing a circle.

❑ The motion is a smooth, flowing circle—hip—pelvis—hip—behind. Only your pelvis moves in an unbroken circle.

❑ Most men find it difficult to sit directly on the bottom of their feet. They can either turn both ankles out towards the floor—this creates a nice little hollow space for their buttocks to rest in. Or they can place the bottom of their toes on the floor and sit on their heels, which will then be facing up towards the ceiling.

Repetitions
IN EACH DIRECTION
WORK UP TO 5

NOTE: Your pelvis can always curl up more than you think it can.

❑ Take a breather for a few seconds, then lift yourself back into position, feeling the stretch in your lower back.

❑ Repeat the Pelvic Rotations, starting to the left.

NOTE: From this angle, you can see how I have taken my buttocks to the back to complete the circle.

DON'TS

❑ **Do not tense your body.**

❑ **Do not shirk when curling your pelvis up. The more you can curl it up into your navel, the more effective this exercise.**

❑ **Do not forget to take breathers whenever you feel it necessary.**

NOTE: At first, some people may experience some discomfort in their knees. Continue to do the exercises very gently, but with your knees slightly apart. Soon the discomfort will subside, unless you have a medical problem.

The Pelvic Scoop

THIS EXERCISE:

- STRENGTHENS THE LEG MUSCLES, ESPECIALLY THE FRONT AND INNER-THIGH MUSCLES, THE STOMACH, BUTTOCKS, AND CALVES •
- STRETCHES THE SPINE•

TECHNIQUE

❑ Kneel on a mat, knees together, with your feet outstretched behind you and your legs relaxed. Keep your arms and shoulders relaxed and your spine straight.

❑ Lift your arms up over your head and clasp your hands together, as far away from you as possible. Feel the stretch in your lower back.

❑ Lower your arms in front about a foot. Round your torso a wee bit forward. Now, keeping your spine straight, aim your buttocks down towards your heels. Do not arch your back.

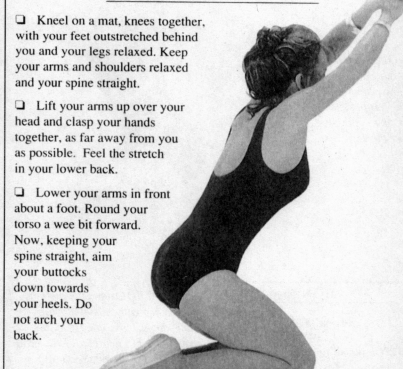

IF THIS EXERCISE IS TOO DIFFICULT:

Only lower your torso towards your heels as much as is comfortable. Do not feel you have to go all the way down.

❏ When you have stretched your buttocks to the point where they are delicately brushing your heels, gently tighten your buttocks, then curl your pelvis up even more than you think you can, in a slow scooping motion.

❏ Raise your arms back up till your hands are above your head in the starting position.

❏ Keep curling your pelvis up until you have returned to the original kneeling position. When your pelvis is curled up, your buttocks will be closer to your heels.

Repetitions
WORK UP TO 10

NOTE: The stronger you are, the more you will be able to take your arms towards the back when you are scooping back up. Also, the more you can take your arms and torso back when you are returning to the original kneeling position with your curl-up, the faster your thigh muscles will strengthen. This is, however, quite a challenge. And the higher you can curl your pelvis, the more you will be strengthening your inner thighs.

*Do not strain your calves. If you feel a strain or pull in your
calves when you are returning to the starting position,
bend your arms and torso forward. After doing
this scoop regularly you will soon be able
to relax your calves without
thinking about it.*

FOR MORE OF A CHALLENGE:
Push your knees together when
you are returning to the
starting position.

DON'TS

❑ Do not tense your body.

❑ Do not strain your arms forward, and keep your arms and shoulders relaxed.

❑ Do not uncurl your pelvis when you are returning to your original kneeling position.

❑ Do not arch your back when aiming your buttocks towards your heels.

❑ Do not let your buttocks untighten when you are returning to the kneeling position.

❑ Do not keep on going relentlessly. If you find yourself needing a breather, take one. Relax your body and breathe naturally. Then resume the original position and continue.

The Pelvic Rotation—Figure of 8

This exercise is done in exactly the same manner as the Pelvic Rotation working the same muscles, but harder. This time the motion is a smooth figure 8—one hip up—the opposite buttock down and back—one hip up—the opposite buttock down and back. Only your pelvis moves. Only attempt this exercise after you have become very strong from doing the Pelvic Rotation and the Pelvic Scoop.

TECHNIQUE

❑ Sit on your heels, knees together, your legs relaxed.

❑ Lift your arms up over your head and clasp your hands together. Feel the stretch in your lower back, and keep your torso erect.

❑ Lift your torso 2 to 3 inches up off your heels, or higher if this is uncomfortable.

❑ Take your right hip out to the side, as far as you can. Then roll your right hip forward, aiming it up. As you do this, your left hip will automatically lower a few inches, and be aimed more towards your back.

❑ Then, take your left buttock back as far as it will go. When your left buttock cannot go back any further, gently start rounding your left hip forward in a half-circle to the point where your left hip is up and forward as far as it can go. Your right hip is now back.

DON'TS

❑ Do not arch your back or stick out your buttocks.

❑ Do not tense your body.

Repetitions

WORK UP TO 5

51

The Front-Thigh Stretch

THIS EXERCISE:

• STRETCHES THE NECK, PECTORAL MUSCLES, SPINE AND THIGHS •

• STRENGTHENS THE BUTTOCKS, INNER THIGHS AND STOMACH •

TECHNIQUE

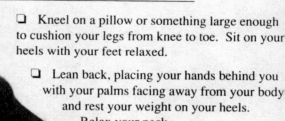

❏ Kneel on a pillow or something large enough to cushion your legs from knee to toe. Sit on your heels with your feet relaxed.

❏ Lean back, placing your hands behind you with your palms facing away from your body and rest your weight on your heels. Relax your neck.

❏ Still sitting on your heels, tighten your buttocks. Curl your pelvis up more than you think you can. Then curl it up even more. Now, lift your buttocks up off your heels no more than 1 inch. Do not arch your back. The more you can curl your pelvis up, the more your thigh muscles will stretch to give them a long, sleek, tight look.

❏ If you can't reach behind you at first, rest your hands by your sides.

NOTE: The picture opposite, bottom is the starting position. Notice that there is less of a curve in the lower back and that the pubis bone can be seen in this picture. This shows how much the pelvis is curled up. Keep your knees together and your shoulders relaxed. Your pelvis should be curled up, even when sitting on your heels. It may be more comfortable for you in the beginning to separate your knees a wee bit.

Repetitions
WORK UP TO **10**

❏ Move gently up and down no more than ¼ to ½ inch.

DON'TS

❏ Do not arch your back. Keep your spine straight.

❏ Do not tense your neck.

❏ Do not move your head up or down.

❏ Do not forget to curl your pelvis up. The more you do this, the more your thighs will stretch.

❏ Do not put too much pressure on your hands and do not lock your elbows. Your arms should be straight but relaxed.

❏ Do not tense your body.

BUILD YOUR STRENGTH

The following programme has been devised to help you slowly increase your strength if you find the Quick Callanetics or Advanced Exercises programmes too much for you at first.

The Underarm Tightener, Waist-Away Stretch and the Neck Relaxer act as a general warm up to loosen your body before moving on to the more specific exercises aimed at working your hips and behind.

Days 1-4

The Underarm Tightener

It may not be anatomically proper, but underarm is the best term I've found to describe the under part of the upper arm— the part that tends to get loose and dangling. This exercise will help to banish underarm goosh.

THIS EXERCISE:
- EXPANDS AND STRETCHES THE CHEST •
- TIGHTENS THE UNDERARMS •
- STRETCHES THE SPINE AND PECTORAL MUSCLES •
- LOOSENS AND RELIEVES TENSION IN
  THE NECK AND THE AREA BETWEEN
  THE SHOULDER BLADES •

❑ Sit on the edge of a chair or sofa, keeping your back straight and your feet resting comfortably on the floor. Do not lean back. Take your arms out to the sides. Try to keep them straight, at about shoulder level.

❑ Slowly, turn your hands forward and over, so that the backs of your hands are facing the floor, and your palms and thumbs are facing upward.

❑ Leaning forward, very gently bring your arms back as far as you can, keeping them as straight as possible, as if you were trying to get the backs of your hands to touch. Try to hold your arms as high as possible as you take them back.

DON'TS

❑ **Do not jerk your arms back and forth.**

❑ **Do not arch your back or stick out your stomach.**

❑ **Do not lock your elbows.**

❑ **Do not tense your shoulders.**

❑ Gently, in triple slow motion, move your arms ¼ to ½ inch closer together and back, being very careful to avoid any jerky motions. After a few of these movements, gravity will pull your arms down and your head and shoulders forward from wherever you started. Be conscious of this, and try to return them to the proper position.

❑ You may not be able to keep your elbows entirely straight at first. (Some people are never able to straighten their arms fully; that's perfectly all right.)

Repetitions			
Day 1	Day 2	Day 3	Day 4
25	30	40	50

❑ Upon completion, gently release your arms by bending your elbows and, in triple slow motion, return to the starting position.

The Waist-Away Stretch

An alternative to wearing cinchers and corsets!

THIS EXERCISE:
- STRETCHES THE WAIST, SPINE, BACK OF THE SHOULDERS, AND UNDERARM AREA •
- REDUCES WAIST SIZE •

TECHNIQUE

❏ Sit up straight in an armchair and allow your left arm to rest on the arm of the chair. (If you don't have an armchair, simply rest your left palm beside you on the seat of the chair.)

❏ Keeping the spine straight, slowly stretch your right arm up to the ceiling, palm facing inward. Try to keep your arm by your ear. You should feel the stretch from your waist right up to your underarm. Now, stretch up and try to reach even higher. Then start reaching over gently to the left side, trying to move your upper body and arm in the same direction, as if they were welded together.

❏ When you have reached over to the side as far as you can, move ¼ to ½ inch over and back. You should not be making any bouncing or jerking movements, and remember—move in triple slow motion.

❏ To reverse sides, or to come out of this exercise, slowly lower your arm and straighten your spine, until you have returned to the original position.

NOTE: If you feel any discomfort in your lower back, or if you have a swayback, you may want to try this exercise with your arms and torso bending slightly forward.

DON'TS

❏ Do not bounce.

❏ Do not tense your shoulders or neck.

❏ Do not arch your lower back or stick out your stomach.

R e p e t i t i o n s			
TO EACH SIDE			
Day 1	Day 2	Day 3	Day 4
25	30	40	50

The Neck Relaxer

A way to unlock tension.

THIS EXERCISE:
• LOOSENS THE NECK AND SHOULDERS •
• STRETCHES THE SPINE •
• KEEPS THE NECK AREA FLEXIBLE•

TECHNIQUE

❑ Sit up straight in a chair or stand erect, feet a hip-width apart, knees bent, feet forward. Relax your shoulders—so much so that you feel they are sinking into the floor. Relax your entire body, being careful not to arch your back or stick out your buttocks.

❑ In triple slow motion, stretch your neck up. At the same time, lower your chin until it is resting on your chest. Relax your jaw. Relax your shoulders, and try to keep them even and back.

❑ Gently, leading with your chin, move your head towards your right shoulder until your nose is even with the middle of your shoulder. Now, look over your shoulder as far as possible, trying to stretch your neck even more. Hold for a slow count of 5.

DON'TS

❏ Do not make any sharp or sudden movements; extreme moves can injure your neck.

❏ Do not hunch or tense your shoulders.

❏ Do not tense your jaw; it may help to keep your lips slightly apart.

❏ Do not lock your knees.

❏ Do not stick out your buttocks or stomach.

❏ Neck still stretched, slowly bring your chin back down to your chest and move it towards your left shoulder in one continuous slow motion. Look over your left shoulder as far as possible, as on the right side, holding for a slow count of 5. Slowly, return your head to the centre. This sequence counts as one repetition.

Repetitions TO EACH SIDE			
Day 1	Day 2	Day 3	Day 4
2	2	2	3

61

Bringing Up the Rear (Sitting)

You'll feel this one working!

THE NEXT TWO EXERCISES:

- SCULPT THE BUTTOCKS, GIVING THEM A 'PRECIOUS PEACH' (INSTEAD OF A 'SAGGING PEAR') SHAPE •
- • GET RID OF THE 'JIGGLE' •
- REDUCE SADDLEBAGS, AND EVENTUALLY MAKE THEM DISAPPEAR •
- • STRENGTHEN THE ARM MUSCLES •

TECHNIQUE

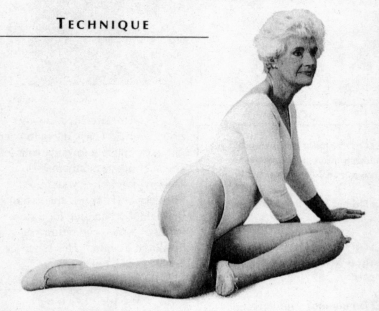

❑ Sit on your left buttock, with your left knee bent, resting comfortably on the floor in front of you, your heel away from your body. Your right leg is out to the side, your right knee bent and even with your left arch. Your right foot is to the back.

❑ Lean your torso to the left and then straighten your back (so that you aren't tempted to arch it). Rest your hands on the floor, anywhere between your knee and hip. Your elbows should be slightly bent.

❑ Lift your right leg so that your knee is several inches off the floor. Gently, in triple slow motion, move your right knee ¼ to ½ inch back and return. After you have completed your repetitions, slowly lower it to the floor.

❑ Reverse and repeat the exercise to the other side.

NOTE: This exercise is based on a ballet position called an attitude. I have modified it so that it works the buttock muscles even more deeply. If you are having trouble raising your leg, move your hands further away from your body and try leaning over to the side more. This will make it easier to lift your leg.

DON'TS

❑ **Do not stick out your buttocks.**

❑ **Do not tense any part of your body, especially your shoulders.**

❑ **Do not push out your stomach.**

❑ **Do not arch your back.**

Repetitions TO EACH SIDE			
Day 1	Day 2	Day 3	Day 4
15	20	25	25

Out to the Side (Sitting)

For a great back view!

TECHNIQUE

*NOTE: After completing the previous
exercise, remember to switch sides
before starting this one.*

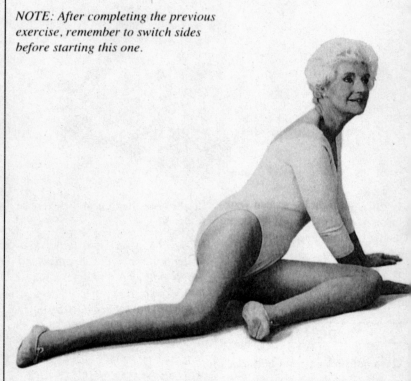

❏ Sit on your left buttock, with your left leg resting comfortably on the
floor in front of you, your knee bent and your heel away from your body.
Your right leg is resting out to the side on the floor, slightly in front of
your hip, knee bent, so that your right knee is even with your left arch.

❏ Lean to your left side and rest your hands on the floor, anywhere
between your knee and hip. Your elbows should be slightly bent.

❏ Lift your right leg as much as you can, but no more than 8 inches off the floor. Gently, move your entire leg up and down ¼ to ½ inch. Alternate sides, working up to the required number of repetitions by breaking it up into sets if you have to.

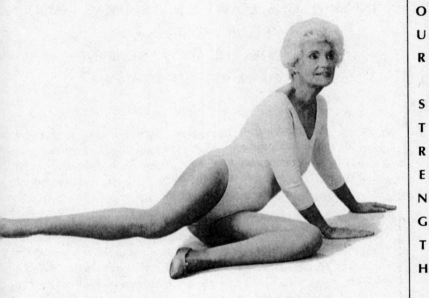

DON'TS
❏ Do not stick out your stomach.
❏ Do not arch your back.
❏ Do not tense your neck or shoulders.

NOTE: Lean to the side as far as necessary to get your legs into the correct position.

Repetitions TO EACH SIDE			
Day1	Day2	Day3	Day4
15	20	25	25

65

The Pelvic Rotation

This exercise and the next are based on a series I learned when studying belly dancing. Everyone loves to show off the flexibility they get from this one in particular. Try it, and you'll see that Elvis had the right idea.

THIS EXERCISE:

- STRENGTHENS THE BUTTOCKS, THIGHS, INNER THIGHS, LOWER BACK, STOMACH, AND PELVIC MUSCLES •
- STRETCHES THE ARMS AND SPINE •
- LOOSENS THE PELVIC AREA •

NOTE: Almost everyone finds this exercise difficult to do at first. This is because pelvic rotations involve most of the muscle groups in your body. You've probably never even used some of them separately, never mind asking them to join together to do something they've never done before! So don't judge yourself; just do the best you can.

Every time you do this exercise, you will be building strength in all these different muscles, and you will start to appreciate the benefits of this beautiful, flowing, seductive movement. Loosening the pelvic area is important. The legs and torso are influenced by it tremendously, and if this area is tight, you won't have the flexibility that everyone is entitled to. This exercise can help you regain the wonderful youthful suppleness and sense of freedom you had as a child.

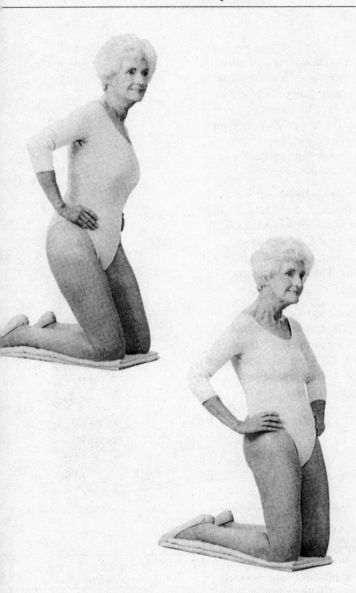

❑ Knees a hip-width apart, kneel on a pillow or something large enough to cushion your legs from knee to foot. Place your hands on your hips and lower your torso 3 inches.

❏ In triple slow motion, gently begin to move your hips (not your torso) as far as you can to the right. Then, slowly, rotate your pelvis to the front. Try to aim your pelvis up towards your navel, then slowly begin to rotate your hips as far as you can to the left side.

❏ Then aim your buttocks to your back, being careful not to arch your lower back, but rather trying to stretch to your back so that you feel the stretch in the lower part of your spine. This completes one movement.

❏ Working at your own pace, complete the repetitions to this side, circling to the right, front, left, and back. Then take a breather if you feel you need it before reversing direction.

DON'TS

❏ **Do not arch your back.**

❏ **Do not stick out your stomach.**

❏ **Do not try to do too much too fast.**

Repetitions TO EACH SIDE			
Day1	Day2	Day3	Day4
2	**2**	**2**	**2**

The Pelvic Scoop

Graceful, flowing...beautifying.

THIS EXERCISE:

- STRENGTHENS THE LEG MUSCLES, ESPECIALLY THE FRONT AND INNER-THIGH MUSCLES, THE STOMACH, BUTTOCKS, AND CALVES •
- STRETCHES THE SPINE•

TECHNIQUE

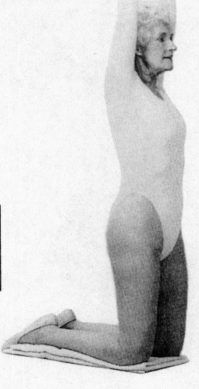

❏ Knees a hip-width apart, kneel on a pillow or something large enough to cushion your legs from knee to foot.

❏ Try to bring your arms straight up over your head, clasp your hands, and try to stretch your upper body, including your neck, as if you were trying to make your torso longer. Do this to the point where you can feel your lower back stretching.

DON'TS

❏ Do not arch your back.

❏ Do not jerk up your pelvis.

❏ Continue to stretch as you slowly lower your buttocks about 4 inches, then tighten your buttock muscles and slowly curl up your pelvis. Hold this position for a count of three. Your arms will move forward when you curl the pelvis.

❏ In triple slow motion, still curling up your pelvis, use the strength of your thighs to lift your body back to the starting position. Try to keep stretching your spine as you do these slow, sinuous, powerful movements.

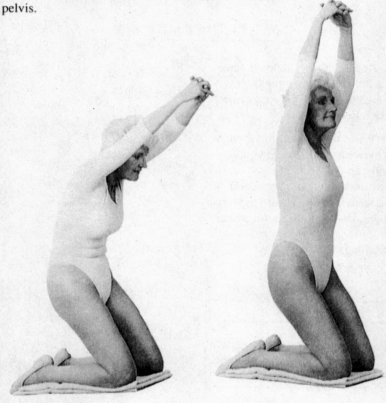

Repetitions			
Day 1	Day 2	Day 3	Day 4
2	2	2	2

The Front-Thigh Stretch

For tight, slim, beautiful thighs.

THIS EXERCISE:

- STRETCHES THE NECK, PECTORAL MUSCLES, SPINE, AND THIGHS •
- STRENGTHENS THE BUTTOCKS, INNER THIGHS, AND STOMACH •

TECHNIQUE

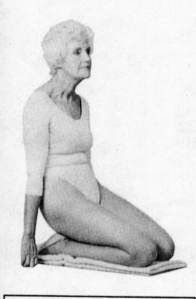

❑ Kneel on a pillow or something large enough to cushion your legs from knee to toe. Place your knees together and sit back on your heels. Support yourself by making fists with your hands and place them on the floor at your sides, so that they are even with your toes.

❑ Still on your heels, tighten your buttocks and curl up your pelvis. Hold this position for the count.

❑ Return to the original position by releasing your buttocks and, still sitting on your heels, using your fists to walk yourself to an upright position. Relax.

DON'TS

❑ Do not arch your back or stick out your stomach.

❑ Do not tense your body.

❑ Do not hunch your shoulders.

Hold for a count of...			
Day 1	Day 2	Day 3	Day 4
10	10	15	15

The Spine Stretch

To release those muscles you've been working so hard.

THIS EXERCISE:

• STRETCHES THE ENTIRE BACK, SPINE, BETWEEN THE SHOULDER BLADES, PECTORALS, BUTTOCKS, HIPS, AND OUTER THIGHS •

TECHNIQUE

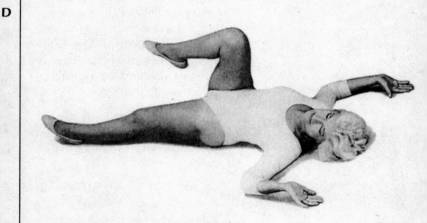

❑ Lie on the floor, knees bent, feet flat on the floor a hip-width apart. Extend your arms out at shoulder level, elbows bent up at right angles, so that the backs of your hands rest on the floor.

❑ Bring your right knee towards your chest. Slide your left foot forward so that your leg is fully extended on the floor. Keeping your right leg bent, bring it over to your left as far as you can, so that your right foot is resting on your left leg, anywhere that is comfortable except directly on top of the kneecap.

❏ Allow gravity to lower your right knee as close to the floor as possible, keeping your right leg relaxed. Try to keep your shoulders and elbows on the floor. Hold for the count.

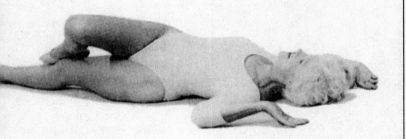

❏ To come out of this position, in triple slow motion return your bent right knee to your chest and then slowly lower your right foot to the floor keeping the knee bent.

❏ Bring your left leg to your chest and repeat on the other side.

NOTE: If your muscles are stretched enough, after a count of ten, still resting your foot on the extended leg, move the bent knee toward the floor and back no more than ¼ of an inch in triple slow motion 15 times.

Like Lucy in the picture, you may have trouble at first getting the backs of your hands to lie flat against the floor.

Hold for a count of... TO EACH SIDE			
Day1	Day2	Day3	Day4
25	25	25	25

DON'TS

❏ **Do not lift your shoulders off the floor.**

❏ **Do not bring your elbows off the floor.**

❏ **Do not turn your head to either side.**

❏ **Do not jerk your bent knee.**

❏ **Do not force the stretch.**

73

Days 5-9

The Underarm Tightener

TECHNIQUE

❏ Repeat the exercise as for Days 1-4, trying to keep your head and body as erect as possible. Hold your arms up as high as you can. You may find that, sitting straight, you cannot raise your arms as high as you did for Days 1-4. If your chair has a high back, you'll need to straddle it backward, as pictured, to keep it from getting in your way.

NOTE: The more you rotate your arms, the more your palms face upward, and the higher your arms are held, the more you will feel this exercise and the faster it will work!

DON'TS

❑ Do not jerk your arms back and forth.

❑ Do not arch your back or stick out your stomach.

❑ Do not lock your elbows.

❑ Do not tense your shoulders.

Repetitions				
Day 5	Day 6	Day 7	Day 8	Day 9
30	40	50	60	75

The Waist-Away Stretch

TECHNIQUE

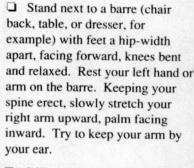

❏ Stand next to a barre (chair back, table, or dresser, for example) with feet a hip-width apart, facing forward, knees bent and relaxed. Rest your left hand or arm on the barre. Keeping your spine erect, slowly stretch your right arm upward, palm facing inward. Try to keep your arm by your ear.

❏ Still stretching upward, tighten your buttocks and curl up your pelvis. Then start reaching over to the left side. Complete the exercise as for Days 1-4, bending both knees deeply as you come out of the position.

❏ Work both sides.

NOTE: At first you may have to do this exercise bent slightly forward, and you may not be able to keep the raised arm straight or by your ear. As you get stronger, your torso will be able to stretch over to the side more, and instead of just feeling the stretch in your waist, you will feel it from your hip to your hand!

DON'TS

❏ Do not bounce.

❏ Do not tense your shoulders or neck.

❏ Do not arch your lower back or stick out your stomach.

❏ Do not lock your knees.

R e p e t i t i o n s
TO EACH SIDE

Day 5	Day 6	Day 7	Day 8	Day 9
30	40	50	60	75

The Neck Relaxer

TECHNIQUE

DON'TS

❏ **Do not make any sharp or sudden movements.**

❏ **Do not hunch or tense your shoulders.**

❏ **Do not tense your jaw.**

❏ **Do not lock your knees.**

❏ **Do not stick out your stomach or arch your back.**

❏ Repeat as for Days 1-4. If you have been doing this exercise sitting down, now do it standing, with knees bent. As your muscles relax and become stretched you will find that you can stretch further without tensing your shoulders.

Repetitions TO EACH SIDE				
Day 5	Day 6	Day 7	Day 8	Day 9
3	3	3	3	3

Bringing Up the Rear (Sitting)

TECHNIQUE

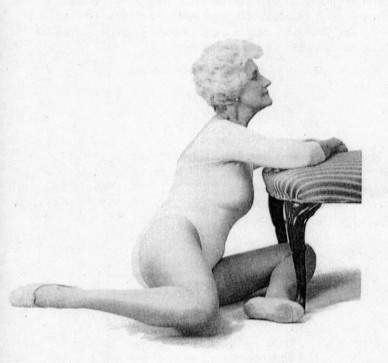

❏ In front of a sofa or chair, sit on your left buttock with your left knee bent and resting comfortably on the floor in front of you, your heel several inches away from your body. Your right leg is out to the side, knee bent and even with your right hip, if possible. Your toes should be relaxed and pointing to the back.

❏ Rest your elbows and forearms on the seat of the chair or sofa and lean your torso over to the left. Lift your right leg so that your knee is a few inches off the floor, still trying to keep it even with your right hip. Gently, in triple slow motion, move your right knee ¼ to ½ inch to the back, then return it even with the hip.

❏   After you have completed your repetitions, slowly lower your leg to the floor.

❏   If you find that your muscles are not strong enough to support this motion, or you cannot do it without leaning your torso forward or arching your lower back, then lean your torso even further to the left—as far as you need to. Once the buttock muscles are strong enough, you will be able to straighten up your torso gradually.

❏   Reverse and repeat the exercise to the other side.

NOTE: If you are raising your leg too high and aiming your knee upward, you will be working the front-thigh muscles more than your buttocks. Instead of compensating in this way, lean your torso further to the side or take a breather. This is a sign that the buttock muscles may be weak.

DON'TS

❏ Do not stick out your buttocks.

❏ Do not tense any part of your body, especially your shoulders.

❏ Do not push out your stomach.

❏ Do not arch your back.

Repetitions TO EACH SIDE				
Day 5	Day 6	Day 7	Day 8	Day 9
30	35	40	45	50

Out to the Side (Sitting)

TECHNIQUE

❑ Repeat as for Days 1-4, but this time take the extended leg directly out to the side, so that it is as even with your hip as possible. Try to straighten the extended leg so that your foot, knee, and hip are even, but do not force it. Lift your leg no more than 6 to 8 inches off the floor.

❑ Work both sides.

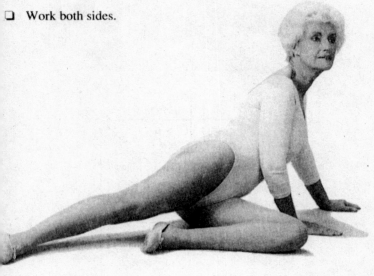

NOTE: If your buttock muscles are not strong enough to support this motion, or you cannot do it without arching your back, lean as far over to the side opposite the extended leg as you need to, making sure that the lower back is stretched so that you don't put any pressure on it. Once your muscles are strong enough, you will be able to straighten your torso gradually and lift your leg with ease.

Repetitions TO EACH SIDE				
Day 5	Day 6	Day 7	Day 8	Day 9
30	35	40	45	50

DON'TS

❏ Do not stick out your stomach.

❏ Do not arch your back.

❏ Do not tense your neck or shoulders.

❏ Do not lock your knee.

The Pelvic Rotation

TECHNIQUE

❏ Repeat as for Days 1-4, but this time bring your arms straight up over your head, clasp your hands and try to stretch your whole upper torso to the point where you can feel the stretch in your lower back. Then lower your body 6 inches, and continue as for Days 1-4.

NOTE: When you begin, do these motions in triple slow motion. As you become more adept, you can gradually increase your pace.

DON'TS

❏ Do not arch your back.

❏ Do not stick out your stomach.

❏ Do not try to do too much too fast.

Repetitions IN EACH DIRECTION				
Day 5	Day 6	Day 7	Day 8	Day 9
3	3	3	3	3

The Pelvic Scoop

TECHNIQUE

NOTE: As you become more adept at this exercise, you won't have to lean forward and will be able to keep your shoulders back even more as you come up.

❑ From the starting position, stretch your arms and torso as for Days 1-4. Continue to stretch as you aim your buttocks towards your heels. Round and lean your torso forward while slowly lowering your buttocks, as if you were going to sit down. Aim toward your heels and make sure you do not arch your back.

❑ Lower yourself about 6 to 8 inches, then tighten your buttock muscles and slowly curl up your pelvis. Return to the starting position using the strength of your thighs as for Days 1-4.

DON'TS

❑ Do not arch your back.

❑ Do not jerk up your pelvis.

Repetitions				
Day5	Day6	Day7	Day8	Day9
3	3	3	3	3

The Front-Thigh Stretch

TECHNIQUE

❏ Repeat as for Days 1-4, but this time, instead of making fists with your hands, try to place your palms on the floor behind you.

NOTE: This movement will seem easier if you try to stay conscious of relaxing your entire body as you do it.

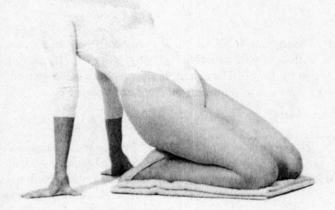

Hold for a count of...				
Day5	Day6	Day7	Day8	Day9
20	20	20	20	20

DON'TS

❏ Do not arch your back or stick out your stomach.

❏ Do not tense your body.

❏ Do not hunch your shoulders.

The Spine Stretch

TECHNIQUE

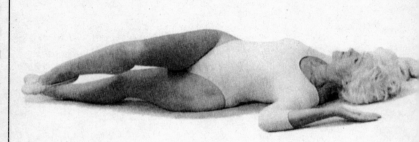

❑ Repeat as for Days 1-4, but as you take your knee over, bring your foot with it, in front of your extended leg. Let your leg dangle, as close to the floor as gravity pulls it. Then, in triple slow motion, move your right knee no more than ¼ an inch towards the floor and back.

❑ Work both sides.

DON'TS

❑ Do not lift your shoulders off the floor.

❑ Do not bring your elbows off the floor.

❑ Do not turn your head to either side.

❑ Do not jerk the bent knee.

❑ Do not force the stretch.

NOTE: Be sure that your shoulders and elbows do not come off the floor. You will get the greatest benefit from this stretch, especially in the area of the lower back, if you concentrate on keeping your shoulders and elbows down, rather than bringing your knee down.

Repetitions TO EACH SIDE				
Day 5	Day 6	Day 7	Day 8	Day 9
15	20	25	30	30

The Underarm Tightener

TECHNIQUE

❏ Repeat as for Days 1-4. But this time try the exercise standing erect, your feet a hip-width apart, your knees bent. Each day you do this exercise, try to keep your arms as high as possible, behind you, with your shoulders and head held back.

NOTE: When you first attempt this exercise, you may find that your head and shoulders round forward and that it is difficult to keep your buttocks from sticking out. As you become stronger, you will be able to stand more and more erect.

DON'TS

❏ **Do not jerk your arms back and forth.**

❏ **Do not arch your back or stick out your stomach.**

❏ **Do not lock your elbows.**

❏ **Do not tense your shoulders.**

❏ **Do not lock your knees.**

Repetitions						
Day 10	Day 11	Day 12	Day 13	Day 14	Day 15	Day 16
50	50	55	60	65	75	75

B
U
I
L
D

Y
O
U
R

S
T
R
E
N
G
T
H

The Waist-Away Stretch

TECHNIQUE

❑ Repeat as for Days 5-9, but this time, instead of resting your arm on a barre, support yourself by placing your hand just below your hip, your elbow pointing straight out to the side, if possible, and straighten your knees a bit.

❑ Slowly stretch your other arm upward, palm facing inward. Stretch up and over to the side, trying to move your upper body and arm together. You may bend slightly forward if necessary. Continue as for Days 5-9.

❏ To reverse sides, keep your hand on your hip and bend your knees even more. Continue to stretch the right arm over, and continue around to the front, slowly extending your arm down and then over to the right side in a slow sweeping movement. Coming out of the stretch in this way prevents putting pressure on the lower back.

❏ Tighten your buttocks, curl up your pelvis, and slowly straighten your spine, vertebra by vertebra, as you lower the arm. Repeat the exercise on the left side. When you have completed the left side, come out of the exercise as above.

NOTE: At first you may have trouble keeping your arm fully extended and curling your pelvis up.

DON'TS

❏ Do not bounce.

❏ Do not tense your shoulders or neck.

❏ Do not arch your lower back or stick out your stomach.

❏ Do not let your resting elbow point forward or backward.

❏ Do not lock your knees.

Repetitions TO EACH SIDE						
Day 10	Day 11	Day 12	Day 13	Day 14	Day 15	Day 16
50	50	55	60	65	75	75

The Neck Relaxer

TECHNIQUE

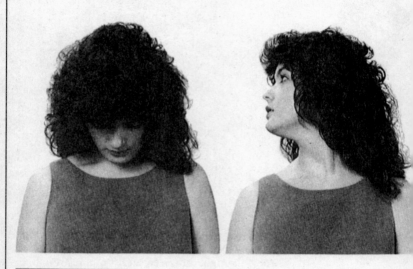

DON'TS

❏ Do not make any sharp or sudden movements.

❏ Do not hunch or tense your shoulders.

❏ Do not tense your jaw.

❏ Do not lock your knees.

❏ Do not stick out your buttocks or stomach.

❏ Repeat as for Days 5-9, but this time, at the same time, curl up your pelvis as far as you can, to stretch your spine.

Repetitions
TO EACH SIDE

Day 10	Day 11	Day 12	Day 13	Day 14	Day 15	Day 16
3	3	3	3	3	3	3

Bringing Up the Rear (Sitting)

TECHNIQUE

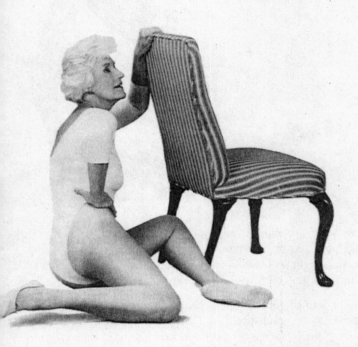

❏ Position yourself as for Days 5-9, this time holding on to a barre (a sofa or chair, a table, or anything else strong enough to support you) with your left hand. Place your right hand on your right hip.

DON'TS

❏ Do not stick out your buttocks.

❏ Do not tense any part of your body, especially your shoulders.

❏ Do not push out your stomach.

❏ Do not arch your back.

NOTE: Work up to the required number of repetitions by breaking it up into sets and switching from side to side, or taking breathers, if you have to.

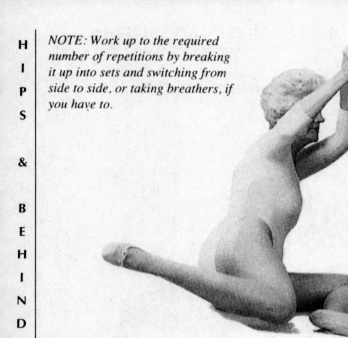

❑ Rotate your right hip forward, rolling it over as far as it will go with your right hand, so that both hips are even with each other and facing forward. Your right foot should come off the floor, higher than the knee. If it doesn't, lift it up with your right hand.

❑ Trying not to let your hip roll back, put your right hand on the barre. Leaning over to the opposite side as far as you need to, lift your right knee no more than 4 inches off the floor, keeping the knee even with your right hip.

❑ Keeping your foot higher than your knee, gently move your knee ¼ to ½ inch back, then return. Do not let your knee come forward more than it did in the starting position. After you have completed your repetitions, slowly lower your leg to the floor.

❑ Reverse and repeat to the other side.

Repetitions TO EACH SIDE						
Day 10	Day 11	Day 12	Day 13	Day 14	Day 15	Day 16
50	55	60	65	70	75	75

Out to the Side (Sitting)

TECHNIQUE

❏ Position yourself as for Days 5-9, but this time sit in front of and hold on to the barre with your left hand, and place your foot further from your body. Using your right hand, gently rotate your right hip forward.

❏   Then grasp the barre with both hands, lean over to the side if you have to in order to lift your leg from 1 to 3 inches, and continue as for Days 5-9, straightening your working leg as far as you can.

❏   Work both sides.

DON'TS

❏ Do not stick out your stomach.

❏ Do not arch your back.

❏ Do not tense your neck or shoulders.

❏ Do not lock your knees.

NOTE: Remember to take your leg directly out to the side, in line with your hip. It is a common tendency to want to take the leg forward, but this will not get the results you want.

Repetitions TO EACH SIDE						
Day 10	Day 11	Day 12	Day 13	Day 14	Day 15	Day 16
50	55	60	65	70	75	75

The Pelvic Rotation

TECHNIQUE

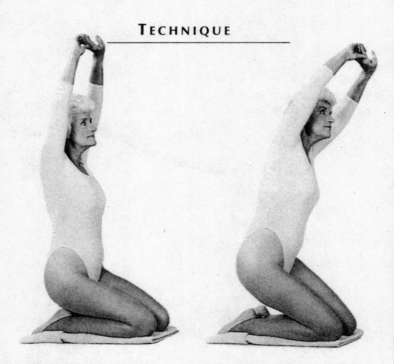

❏ Knees together, sit back on your heels, keeping your spine straight. Bring your arms over your head as for Days 5-9. Now, lift your body straight up about 4 inches off your heels, or higher if you have to. Continue to rotate your pelvis as for Days 1-4.

❏ Repeat in the opposite direction.

NOTE: It is important to remember to work at your own pace, taking breathers whenever you need them.

DON'TS

❏ Do not arch your back.

❏ Do not stick out your stomach.

❏ Do not try too much too fast.

Repetitions IN EACH DIRECTION						
Day 10	Day 11	Day 12	Day 13	Day 14	Day 15	Day 16
4	4	4	4	4	4	4

95

The Pelvic Scoop

TECHNIQUE

❑ Repeat as for Days 5-9, but with your knees together. Lower your body 8 to 10 inches.

NOTE: As you become more adept at this exercise, your movements will become more fluid. You will be able to keep your knees together easily and learn to relax your calf muscles.

DON'TS

❑ Do not arch your back.

❑ Do not jerk up your pelvis.

Repetitions						
Day 10	Day 11	Day 12	Day 13	Day 14	Day 15	Day 16
4	4	4	4	4	4	4

The Front-Thigh Stretch

TECHNIQUE

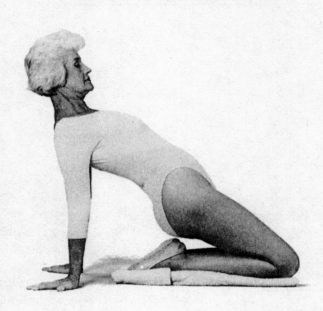

❑ Repeat as for Days 5-9. When you have stretched enough to feel a slight pull in the front of your thighs, curl up your pelvis even more and lift your buttocks off your heels, no more than one inch at first. Hold this position for the count.

❑ Relax your buttocks and gently return to the starting position, sitting on your heels. Relax your entire body.

DON'TS

❑ Do not arch your back or stick out your stomach.

❑ Do not allow your head to drop back.

❑ Do not tense your body.

❑ Do not hunch your shoulders or tense your neck.

Hold for a count of...						
Day 10	Day 11	Day 12	Day 13	Day 14	Day 15	Day 16
30	30	30	30	30	30	30

97

The Spine Stretch

TECHNIQUE

DON'TS

❏ Do not lift your shoulders off the floor.

❏ Do not bring your elbows off the floor.

❏ Do not turn your head to either side.

❏ Do not jerk the bent knee.

❏ Do not force the stretch.

❏ Repeat as for Days 5-9, but try to touch your right toe to the floor. Continue as for Days 5-9, moving your right knee ¼ of an inch closer to the floor and back.

❏ Work both sides.

NOTE: As your muscles begin to stretch, you will enjoy doing this exercise more and more— I promise!

	Repetitions TO EACH SIDE						
	Day 10	Day 11	Day 12	Day 13	Day 14	Day 15	Day 16
	30	35	35	35	40	40	40

Days 17-30

The Underarm Tightener

TECHNIQUE

❏ Repeat as for Days 10-16, this time tightening your buttocks and curling up your pelvis, your knees only slightly bent. Try to hold your arms up even higher than before.

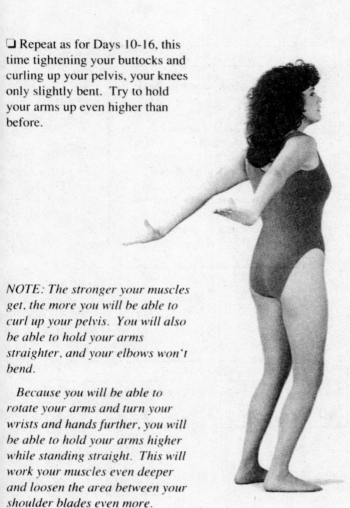

NOTE: The stronger your muscles get, the more you will be able to curl up your pelvis. You will also be able to hold your arms straighter, and your elbows won't bend.

Because you will be able to rotate your arms and turn your wrists and hands further, you will be able to hold your arms higher while standing straight. This will work your muscles even deeper and loosen the area between your shoulder blades even more.

DON'TS

❏ Do not jerk your arms back and forth.

❏ Do not arch your back or stick out your stomach.

❏ Do not lock your elbows.

❏ Do not tense your shoulders.

❏ Do not lock your knees.

Repetitions						
Day 17	Day 18	Day 19	Day 20	Day 21	Day 22	Days 23-30
60	70	75	75	75	75	75

The Waist-Away Stretch

TECHNIQUE

❑ Repeat as for Days 10-16, standing straight and tightening your buttocks and curling up the pelvis even more before you start reaching over to the side. Try to hold your extended arm by your ear.

❑ Work both sides.

DON'TS

❑ Do not bounce.

❑ Do not tense your shoulders or neck.

❑ Do not arch your lower back or stick out your stomach.

❑ Do not let your resting elbow point forward or backward.

❑ Do not lock your knees.

NOTE: As your muscles get stronger, you will find that you can curl up your pelvis and bend over to the side even more. You will gradually be able to straighten your legs, still keeping them relaxed, and you will be able to keep your arms straight and by your ear. You will also become even more conscious of the wonderful stretch in your spine.

Repetitions TO EACH SIDE						
Day 17	Day 18	Day 19	Day 20	Day 21	Day 22	Days 23-30
60	70	75	75	75	75	75

The Neck Relaxer

TECHNIQUE

❏ Repeat as for Days 10-16, trying to curl up your pelvis even more, and without bending your knees as much.

DON'TS

❏ Do not make any harsh or sudden movements.

❏ Do not hunch or tense your shoulders.

❏ Do not tense your jaw.

❏ Do not lock your knees.

❏ Do not stick out your stomach or arch your back.

Repetitions
TO EACH SIDE

Day 17	Day 18	Day 19	Day 20	Day 21	Day 22	Days 23-30
3	3	3	3	3	3	3

Bringing Up the Rear (Sitting)

TECHNIQUE

❑ Repeat as for Days 10-16, trying to sit straighter and not lean your torso so far to the side. On your working leg, try to keep the foot level with the knee, no higher, to really work the buttock muscles.

NOTE: As your muscles become stronger, you will be able to do this exercise sitting even straighter. Eventually, you won't have to use your hand to roll your hip forward, and your leg will feel as light as a feather!

DON'TS

❑ **Do not stick out your buttocks.**

❑ **Do not tense any part of your body, especially your shoulders.**

❑ **Do not push out your stomach.**

❑ **Do not arch your back.**

Repetitions
TO EACH SIDE

Day 17	Day 18	Day 19	Day 20	Day 21	Day 22	Days 23-30
75	85	95	100	100	100	100

103

Out to the Side (Sitting)

TECHNIQUE

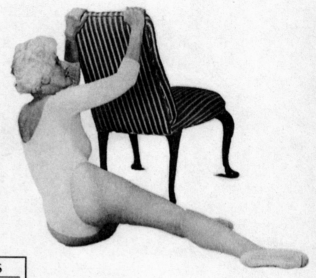

DON'TS

❏ **Do not stick out your stomach.**

❏ **Do not arch your back.**

❏ **Do not let your torso lean forward.**

❏ **Do not lock your knee.**

❏ **Do not tense your neck or shoulders.**

❏ Repeat as for Days 10-16, rotating your hip even further forward, trying to sit more erect, and keeping your working leg straight. Try to turn your leg so that your knee and toes are pointing into the floor, making the buttock muscles work harder.

NOTE: If you find that with your hip rolled forward, you feel your lower back working, round your upper back and shoulders to straighten your spine.

		Repetitions				
		TO EACH SIDE				
Day 17	Day 18	Day 19	Day 20	Day 21	Day 22	Days 23-30
75	85	95	100	100	100	100

The Pelvic Rotation

TECHNIQUE

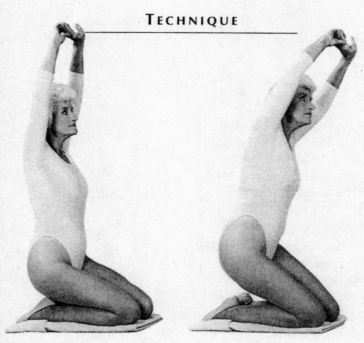

❑ Repeat as for Days 10-16.

NOTE: The stronger you get, the lower you will be able to keep your body and the more you will be able to circle with ease. Soon you will be lifting your body only a few inches off your heels. You will be able to perform this movement smoothly and quickly, taking your hips even further out to the sides and curling up your pelvis even more. With this greater flexibility and range of motion, you will be able to do more repetitions with ease.

DON'TS

❑ Do not arch your back.

❑ Do not stick out your stomach.

❑ Do not try to do too much too fast.

Repetitions
IN EACH DIRECTION

Day 17	Day 18	Day 19	Day 20	Day 21	Day 22	Days 23-30
5	5	5	5	5	5	5

The Pelvic Scoop

TECHNIQUE

❏ Repeat as for Days 10-16, lowering your buttocks as if you were going to sit down until you feel them lightly touch your heels. Tighten your buttock muscles and slowly curl up your pelvis.

❏ Try to straighten your torso and aim your arms straight up; then return to your starting position, making sure you push your knees together, to make the leg muscles work even more.

NOTE: As your muscles strengthen, you will continue to improve until this exercise becomes one flowing, graceful motion.

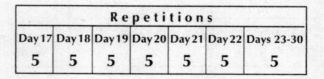

Repetitions						
Day 17	Day 18	Day 19	Day 20	Day 21	Day 22	Days 23-30
5	5	5	5	5	5	5

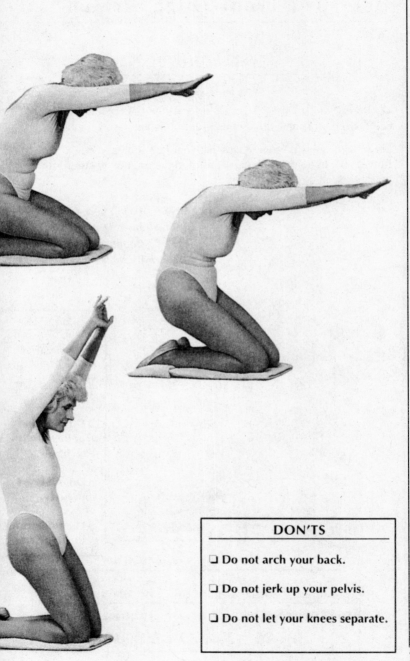

DON'TS

❏ Do not arch your back.

❏ Do not jerk up your pelvis.

❏ Do not let your knees separate.

The Front-Thigh Stretch

TECHNIQUE

❏ Repeat as for Days 10-16. Hold for a count of ten, then curl up your pelvis even more and slowly raise your body half an inch more.

❏ In triple slow motion, gently lift your pelvis up and down ¼ to ½ inch. Release the buttocks and gently return to the original position, sitting on your heels.

NOTE: As you become stronger, you will be able to curl up your pelvis even more, while relaxing your entire body completely.

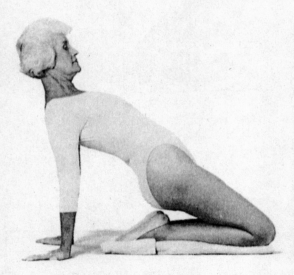

DON'TS

❏ Do not arch your back or stick out your stomach.

❏ Do not allow your head to drop back.

❏ Do not tense your body.

❏ Do not hunch your shoulders.

Repetitions HOLD FOR A COUNT OF 10							
Day 17	Day 18	Day 19	Day 20	Day 21	Day 22	Day 23	Days 24-30
20	20	20	20	30	30	30	40

The Spine Stretch

TECHNIQUE

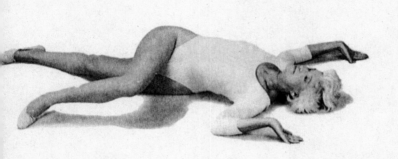

❏ Repeat as for Days 10-16, bringing your knee as close to the floor as possible. Keep your left leg straight on the floor in front of you.

❏ Work both sides.

NOTE: As your muscles stretch, your flexibility will increase and the bent knee will go lower and lower. You may even be able to touch the floor.

DON'TS

❏ Do not lift your shoulders off the floor.

❏ Do not bring your elbows off the floor.

❏ Do not turn your head to either side.

❏ Do not jerk the bent knee.

❏ Do not force the stretch.

Repetitions
TO EACH SIDE

Day 17	Day 18	Day 19	Day 20	Day 21	Day 22	Days 23-30
40	45	45	45	45	45	50